MW00677664

What if you w
law office and you were naked and
didn't know it?

Here's what they're saying nationally and it's no different where you are.

"SUPERB job taking me from a limited policy where I thought I was adequately protected and just wasn't. It is so reassuring to have a specialist who protects me properly for my lawyers professional liability and even saved me thousands of dollars too! Way to go, Mike!"

—Heather Quick
The Quick Law Group, LLC

"They impressed the daylights out of me by showing me where I had major gaps in protection that a specialist with law firms picks up on right away. I would recommend that every lawyer or law firm nationally do a comparison where all of the work is done for you. It's a guaranteed win for you! You haven't found an insurance product ever as great anywhere else!"

—Erik Broel
Broel Law Group, LLC

"It's great not to have to worry that something will go wrong because everything is so efficient. Even in non-crisis situations, the staff is helpful and always get me the best deal on coverage. It's such a relief, under trying circumstances, to deal with people who know how to do their job and seem to have your best interests in mind."

—Scott Ashby
Ashby Law

THE NAKED LAWYER

Leveraging the Lawyers Professional
Liability, Workers Comp, and Office
Business with Data Breach Insurance
Industry to Your Benefit

RJon Robins
Michael Carroll

For reader comments, orders, press and media inquiries:

rjon@howtomanageasmalllawfirm.com
or
michael@insuringlawyer.com

First edition 2012
Second edition 2014
Third edition 2017

ISBN 978-0-9877258-6-8

cover art and all illustrations by Bruce Higdon (bhiggy28@gmail.com)

Acknowledgments

Writing a book for lawyers—our favorite people outside of our own family—has always been a dream of ours, but one that seemed a long shot for two busy entrepreneurs. Then, in the spring of 2014, Michael Carroll attended RJon Robins How To Manage A Small Law Firm Live Quarterly meeting as a guest speaker on the topic of Lawyers Professional Liability. Michael nailed his speech and gave away his First Edition of *The Naked Lawyer* which was well received.

Roughly a year later, RJon approached Michael inquiring to create an exclusive Lawyers Professional Liability program for the 1-10 Lawyers sized firm.

A year later RJon and Michael were able to share "Mission Accomplished" creating a Lawyers Professional Liability exclusive program that is unmatched.

Finally—and this is a long way from formal politeness—Michael & RJon want to express their heartfelt gratitude to their wives Cheryl & Ale. They are their inspiration and their support and always will be.

And you, lawyers, you're the basis of everything we do. Many thanks to you for taking the time to read what we have to say.

Contents

1   It's Not Your Fault...21

2   Could This Happen to You? 27

3   So You Think You Can Never Get Sued? 35

4   Data Breach and Cyber Liability.. 43

5   Income and Outcome... 51

6   Running Errands 59

7   Floods, Earthquakes, Harassment, Discrimination, Termination 65

8   More Than Hurt Feelings 75

9   Lawyers Professional Liability 81

10 People Just Like You 99

Foreword by RJon Robins

I want every lawyer and legal administrator to read this book.

Because the information contained inside, has saved some of the solo and small law firm owners who I know personally, **more than one hundred thousand dollars off the cost of their insurance premiums.** And that's annually!

But I don't even remember when this book was first given to me. Only that it must have been sometime back in the summer of 2012. And that I carried it around with me on a whirlwind tour of the Country as part of **"The National CLE Tour"**, sponsored by Microsoft and LexisNexis, which gave my company the opportunity to meet thousands of lawyers, and share with them some lessons about how to start and build **a more profitable small law firm**. One of which I'll share with you, in here in this introduction.

In fact, I can't even say when or if I would have ever gotten around to reading this book, were it not for a delayed flight between tour stops that had me stranded in some small town I don't even remember where.

And it would have been a real shame had I missed the opportunity to read this book. Because it opened-up for me *a whole new way of understanding* and explaining a better way to think about, negotiate and pay for the *peace of mind* that insurance is *supposed* to bring you.

Of course now that I know what I didn't know then, I wish I had at least documented the arrival at my office, of that thin brown package with my copy of *The Naked Lawyer* inside of it. Together with one of Mike's famous "notes", of course!

If I had understood the effect that this small book would have on my life and business in the coming years I would have saved that thin brown envelope. Sadly, I don't even have the note anymore.

So At This Point You're Probably Wondering Three (3) Things:

1. How can such a small book that you can read in less than 90 minutes have **SUCH A BIG IMPACT** on your life and business?
2. Who am I and how exactly did the information contained in this small book save some lawyers I know well, **more than one hundred thousand dollars** off the cost of their insurance premiums?
3. If the information in this book is so **valuable**, then why did it crisscross the country with me, unread, for nearly a whole year?

The Answer To Question #3 is the easiest of the three to answer so I'll take that one first.

It's because I didn't know, what I didn't know. After all, if I had the ability to know what I do not know yet, then I'd be super-human. But I'm not super-human. I'm just a busy lawyer and business owner, probably a lot like you in many ways.

And in my business, as in yours, there are only *Five (5) Ways To Increase Profits:*

♦ Sell More;
♦ Charge More;
♦ Collect More;
♦ Be More Efficient; and/or
♦ Spend Less.

This book will show you how to spend less. A lot less.

And then every one of those saved-dollars can drop straight to **your bottom line**.

Which brings me to the answer for *Question #1*: **How can such a small book that can be fully-read in less than 90 minutes by an average reader, make such a big difference to your life and business?**

Imagine the most brilliant doctor or engineer or artist who walks into your law office with a legal problem, or an exciting opportunity that calls for a legal solution.

Your prospective new clients are brilliant at what they do. *But they didn't go to law school.* And they don't live in our world of laws and rules of civil or criminal procedure.

In their own world they are masters of their domain. If you or I needed a brilliant doctor, a competent engineer or a creative artist we'd surely be in good hands if we engaged their services. And in our world, they're a lot like a powerful fish that finds itself out of water.

Hopefully, you don't judge them. You don't think they're stupid. In fact, if you study some of the MOST successful rainmakers you will find they have genuine respect for the intelligence and courage it takes for a person who is used to being "large and in-charge" to ask for help when finding him or herself out of their element.

So It's Like This. . .

You and I went to law school. *You probably didn't go to insurance school.* I did. Mike did, too.

Lots of people who don't presume to be any smarter than you, we went to insurance school. And there are things about how to negotiate for insurance coverages and prices, terms and conditions that Mike shares with you in this book that **you have little other chance** of learning about, except the hard way.

Which the hard way also tends to be the expensive way. And the stressful way. And the embarrassing way.

So why would you want to learn about how to buy insurance the hard way, when you can learn practically everything you need to learn to *be an educated consumer of professional insurance products,* just by reading this small book, instead?

EVEN IF YOU DECIDE TO WORK WITH SOMEONE ELSE BESIDES MIKE'S INSURANCE FIRM WE STILL WANT TO *EMPOWER YOU* TO BE AN *EDUCATED CONSUMER* OF PROFESSIONAL INSURANCE PRODUCTS FOR YOUR LAW FIRM.

Here's a fact you will fully appreciate by the time you're done reading this book. I think it's a fact that surprises a lot of smart lawyers who simply didn't go to insurance school. . .

There is no such thing as "an" insurance policy that fully covers a well-run law firm.

Instead, different insurance companies specialize in understanding, pricing and undertaking different types of risk.

You can get "an" insurance policy for malpractice but if you settle just for that you're going to be like the "naked" lawyer on the front cover of this book with his pants down, if anyone working for you is ever engaged in an automobile accident while running an errand on firm business (for example).

In fact, it takes an experienced insurance professional who specializes in law firms to help you think-through AND FIND THE RIGHT BALANCE between all the different areas of exposure you can buy protection for.

The Good News is that an experienced insurance professional should be able to show you how to save enough money on some of the most negotiable of the premiums such that the total bill for FULL COVERAGE often come out about the same or sometimes even less than a poorly priced single-coverage approach.

And I'm not even talking about the BIG COST of getting it wrong!

our Question # 2: Who am I and how exactly did the information contained in this small book save some lawyers I know well, more than one hundred thousand dollars on the cost of their insurance premiums? My name is RJon Robins. I'm a lawyer too. And I learned probably as much as you did in law school about how to buy insurance for a small law firm. . .which is to say I learned nothing.

In 2009 I founded How To Manage a Small Law Firm which today is the largest and also the fastest growing provider of outside "fractional" managing partner services exclusively for solo and small law firms, nationally. You can learn more about that part of my life at our website www.HowToMANAGEaSmallLawFirm.com.

But I think the reason I was selected to write this introduction is that after I went to law school, I also went to insurance school. Yes, as "nerdy" as it sounds I actually find insurance to be a really neat subject. And I find the approach that most insurance companies take to the business of undertaking risk for a fee, to be *absolutely fascinating*.

You see, what most people euphemistically call an insurance "policy" I often refer to as *"a million-dollar, legally binding contract drafted by teams of lawyers funded by billion dollar companies for the express purpose of not paying out a dime, unless absolutely necessary"*. And who can blame them? They undertake enormous risk for relatively small fees all in hopes that you won't screw-up, that your neighbor who they don't even know won't set their office on fire, that your secretary won't rear-end someone in the

car while running to the post office on firm business or that a lighting strike won't put you out of business for a month and they have to cover your operating costs because you spent a few hundred dollars more to buy good business interruption insurance.

So it pays (literally) for you to seek advice from the most experienced insurance professional you can find who has helped thousands of lawyers fashion intelligent insurance strategies that save you money and offer maximum protection, in case "a risk event" ever becomes your new reality.

And finally, the answer to Question #1: How can such a small book that you can read in less than 90 minutes have **SUCH A BIG IMPACT** on your life and business?

It's because an educated consumer of professional insurance products is at a HUGE ADVANTAGE. Plain and simple.

Introduction

reetings and thank you for taking time out of your busy day to read this book. *The Naked Lawyer – Leveraging The Lawyers Professional Liability, Workers Comp, and Office Business with Data Breach Insurance Industry to Your Benefit* was written because we care about lawyers and law firms and want to help you prevent disasters that could potentially put you out of business.

How We Came to be Insurance Specialists for Lawyers and Law Firms

At the outset of Mike's career, he worked for three years at Allstate where he won every award they had to offer. He had one of those Allstate "neighborhood offices" and always thought of himself as an independent insurance broker. He wasn't, of course (he was an employee), but he still held onto that mindset.

Allstate didn't do a lot in the area of commercial insurance—which is what interested him—so he was ready to cut that umbilical cord and go out on his own. It was the best decision he ever made.

The first year on his own he was only 26 years old, his third year out of college—he made over 100 grand. That was a lot of money back in 1990. He put most of it right back into the business to build it up, so he didn't clear much. After two more years, he was up past six figures and never looked back.

During this same period, he became close friends with a family where the father was a successful lawyer and two of his sons also became successful lawyers. They were good people who were well liked and respected. He happened to run into a member of the family who let him know they were unhappy with their present insurance policy. He put him in contact with the older brother who was at that time running the practice. They set an appointment and we wrote up the policy.

It was one of those serendipitous moments in life. He realized how much he really liked lawyers and law firms. Most lawyers have dynamic personalities. They are people who shoot straight, who give you their word and keep their word. They're warm and friendly, fun-loving, and even gregarious. It started him thinking: "These are the kind of people with whom I want to do business *all the time.*"

Once he made this decision, he placed himself under the tutelage of an old-time underwriter and loss-control professional who taught him every nook and cranny of exactly how to *properly* protect lawyers and law firms. Talk about tremendous mentoring—he received it!

Lawyers are busy people. They almost always have a demanding schedule and a practice to run. They don't have time to micro-manage their insurance broker. They are looking for fewer headaches in their life, not more.

It was also clear to him that lawyers and law firms are different, in that he couldn't insure them as he would insure an apartment building. Lawyers and law firms encounter problems and situations that are totally unique to that industry.

It was also clear to him that there were situations that could very quickly put a lawyer or his/her firm completely out of business if not insured correctly. It was because of these potential threats to his clients that he invested the time and effort to become schooled by this loss control / underwriter mentor on every way a lawyer and law firms should be insured. He committed myself at that point to give his future clients the very best that he could offer.

Why This Book

This book is filled to the brim with vivid examples of what can happen to a lawyer and law firms who do not have adequate coverage. These are true stories with names and locations changed. This is a small sampling of the hundreds of horror stories that we've heard through nearly thirty years of working with lawyers and their firms.

We have found that most get their insurance coverage from an insurance broker who would be considered a *generalist*. This type of insurance broker is unaware of the particular needs of the legal profession. Often, they don't know the difference between the specialized needs of a lawyers and those of a strip plaza or a transmission shop. They tend to handle all businesses in the same manner. Their presentation leans toward "one size fits all."

Specialists are as important in the field of insurance as in the medical field—and for the same reason. Whether the medical problem was your own, or someone you cared about, you would attempt to get the best care possible. If you had a heart problem, you would want to be under the care of a heart specialist—hopefully a cardiologist or heart surgeon of proven reputation. A general practitioner would not do.

Our Moral Decision

We're not in business to make certain every law firm is not "insurance poor" through excessive coverage. But we do have a mission to assure that each one is properly protected. Unlike life insurance agents, the commission is around 15%. So if you're concerned that we're dispensing all of this advice to line our pockets, we can demonstrate to you that most of the add-ons discussed in this book make up a very small part of our income. However, the risks in each area addressed hold the potential to ruin your practice. In a sense, our decision is fundamentally a moral one to reveal the inside secrets of how you can leverage the vast resources of this multi-billion-dollar industry for your financial well-being.

As you read through these chapters, ask yourself if the things we describe could happen to you. Do you know for sure that you're covered for any or all of these possible disasters? Stories like these are heart breakers for us because we know that they didn't have to be that way. We've seen millions of dollars lost by unaware lawyers and law firms: lawyers' professional liability, property losses, data beach coverage, employee theft, general liability losses, employment harassment, termination, and discrimination cases and pension plans.

Some of the cases we've witnessed actually resulted in the firms being put out of business.

None of these were our clients—but many subsequently became our clients. It's as though they'd been working away for years stark naked. Today they're fully clothed.

1

it's
NOT
your
FAULT

Lawyers and law firms have been brainwashed about choosing and buying insurance protection!

Stop and think. When you purchased your present insurance coverage, was it from a buddy or a relative or a neighbor down the street? Or did you search the Internet or the Yellow Pages? Did you see a television commercial? Perhaps it was one of your regular customers and you felt you wanted to return the favor. This last is certainly understandable in a business situation.

If any of the above fit your situation, don't think we intend to demean your decision-making procedures. However, for a moment let's compare this to a medical situation.

Similar to the Field of Medicine

As we asked earlier, would you have an eye, ear, nose and throat doctor operate on your knee? Or have a general practitioner perform open heart surgery? You don't just walk into a hospital and accept the first doctor you meet. If a loved one suffered from a disease that even the so-called specialists in your area were not qualified to treat, would you not then see about getting them

to the Mayo Clinic, or a similar center of advanced medicine and treatments? If a case concerns someone you love, the decisions you make will be weighed heavily and you for sure will do your research and check out the doctor's background or history.

Inadvertently Putting Your Law Firm at Risk

Most lawyers that we have come to know look at their practice as a dearly-loved member of the family. For some, their practice has actually *been* a part of the family for three or sometimes four generations. It has provided and still provides for the family for decades. Perhaps you or a member of your family conceived this practice and brought it into being. In any case, it is now your life and your passion and you would never purposely put it in harm's way. Even at the most basic level, you have a security system in place and lock all the doors at night.

Yet many lawyers inadvertently put their practice in danger through simple negligence: they fail to select an insurance broker who is a seasoned specialist in proper insurance for lawyers and law firms.

Obviously, there are insurance brokers in the property and casualty insurance field who have achieved a high degree of success. But the truth is that an insurance broker who is a generalist misses it almost every time when it comes to many of the dangers that we will relate in this book. Of course, they know to cover your business for a fire, a slip and fall, or a tornado. Everyone knows that. But not every insurance broker understands about the hidden law-firm-specific dangers that can put a practice out of business in a matter of days.

We're going to demonstrate that you need a specialist who knows that area of expertise as well as they know anything, an insurance broker who specializes and for whom the legal profession is the number-one business.

Chapter 1

EITHER DO WHAT WE SAY, OR ELSE . . .

Perhaps you've never even thought of your insurance in this way. If that's true, we fully understand. But that's the reason for this book. We want you informed and educated so you will never need to be at risk again. We're here to bring you peace of mind and a better night's sleep.

2 could THIS happen to YOU?

Worse yet, would you even know?

You know your law firm is probably your greatest asset. But did you know it could also be a deadly liability? Did you know that it could cost you more money than you have right now?

Read on

Tony is the managing general partner of a law firm in the Philadelphia area. He began his practice over twenty years ago and has built up a substantial clientele. On this particular morning he was as usual the first to arrive. That was the story of Tony's working life: first to arrive, last to leave.

Tony loved his practice. He loved law. After all, his career represented the American Dream, worth all of the sacrifices.

Something's Wrong

As he walked toward the firm, he picked up litter outside the door. He was a stickler about keeping the place neat as a pin. Opening the door was always a comfort to him. Rather like coming home.

But wait. When he stuck the key in the lock, it didn't feel right. *It was already unlocked.* Someone else must have arrived first for once. But there were no other cars.

He pushed the door open and his heart sank. A quick scan of the premises told him this was going to be bad. Every computer was gone. File cabinets were open. One was knocked over.

Did they take checks? Or did they take any of the firm's confidential client files? His mind started to race. Who could do this sort of thing? Then he saw that his leather chair had been slashed! His heart started pounding with anger—or was it fear? He couldn't be sure. If they'd slashed his chair, that meant they'd done more than steal equipment. They'd vandalized. He knew it wouldn't do much good, but it was time to call the cops.

As he sat there waiting for the police, his mind started to race. What else could they have done? When was the last time he'd conducted a full back-up of computer files?

Tony wandered back to the supply room. "Holy smokes!" he moaned. "Look at how much they took!"

What would he tell his clients that day? What would he tell the other lawyers and the employees? How long would it take to get back to business?

His computer tech supposedly had back-up systems in place, yet what if he was on a scheduled job and couldn't come right over? Would Tony have to wait almost a week before he was fully up and running? As the cold, hard facts began to settle in on him, Tony realized this could mean an incredible loss of revenue.

Panic Sets In

His thoughts then turned to his insurance broker. He had never paid much attention to that policy. Always figured nothing would really go wrong. Now he really felt panicky. What was covered? What wasn't? How would he pay the bills while the practice was down? Would he have to lay people off?

His mind turned to the people on his payroll, Might one of them have done this? "No! Couldn't be. I've treated them like family."

He heard a knock on the door. The cops.

It took a few missed phone calls, but finally Tony caught up with his insurance broker, Jim. Tony relayed to Jim the whole sad story. The next day, the assigned insurance adjuster named Alan came down to the law firm and walked through it with Tony. At the end of their tour Tony looked at Alan expectantly. "Well?"

He could tell by the look on Alan's face there was something wrong. Alan's eyes were darting around the room.

"Tony, I'm afraid we might have some problems."

"What problems? All insurance policies cover theft, right?"
"That's true, Tony. Theft *is* covered. But as you'll see if you read your policy carefully, there *are* exclusions. In fact, your policy doesn't cover computers and other office machines. There's no provision for the restoration of damaged property and. . .something else. Oh yeah, there are also limitations on some items that are actually covered."

Unprepared and Uninformed

As it turns out, Tony wasn't as prepared for this unfortunate event as he had thought. As a result, Jim is no longer Tony's insurance broker.

Tony was crushed. The law firm was his life. It represented his security and his freedom. Someday it would be his retirement. A thing like this could screw it all up for years.

Can you relate?

We're here to say, "It doesn't have to be this way!"

You can have the dreams you cherish. You can count on the security you desire. You don't have to worry every day about something happening that's going to set you back.

What Can Go Wrong?

We know it's not just vandalism or theft. A lot goes wrong around a law firms just because that's the way it is. It's the nature of business.

Let's say a fire starts in the business next door. Your firm suffers smoke damage and your sprinklers went off too. Who's responsible? Are you covered?

Let's take the scenario a bit further. Say this fire puts you out of business for a month. At this point

◆ Who pays your employees?
◆ Who pays your fixed bills?
◆ Who pays your electricity, phone, water?
◆ Do you have enough cash flow to survive?
◆ Who pays you?

Or will you go out of business for something that was completely out of your control? It doesn't seem fair, does it?

WHY WOULD SOMEONE DO THIS TO *ME?*

We've seen good people suffer needlessly because they didn't know the secrets of how to make the huge resources of the insurance industry work for them. We've been working with lawyers and law firms for a long time and we've heard every horror story in the book.

If Tony had been our client, his problem would have been taken care of quickly and easily. Many times, lawyers like Tony's became our clients *after* they had a really serious claim. They often express the wish that they'd come to us— insurance specialists—*before* the claim.

Tony Learns the Inside Secrets

A few weeks after the break-in, Tony met with us for a serious talk and the next time we got together he was beaming like a man who'd seen the light. We knew this was the case the moment he opened the conversation.

"Mike & RJon, you really told me the inside secrets of the insurance industry. I usually hate paperwork but I'm a businessman and I *do* have my life invested in this Firm. I now know more about protecting my practice and the future for myself and my family more than I ever thought was possible."

In one short meeting, we had shown Tony:

♦ How to avoid the single biggest mistake lawyers and law firms make in protecting their practice.
♦ The importance of having a broad market of insurers to get the most complete coverage at the best price.
♦ The importance of having a risk analysis on your law firm.
♦ The importance of having a risk management program for your law firm and the simplest way to start one.
♦ The most powerful, proven, 7-step system for protecting your law firm and your future.

After his meeting with us, Tony simply felt more confident. One meeting completely took away the cloud of uncertainty that had been hanging over his head for so long. Now he enjoyed peace of mind.

Are you reading this and wishing you also had access to this kind of information? Good news! That's exactly what *The Naked Lawyer* is all about.

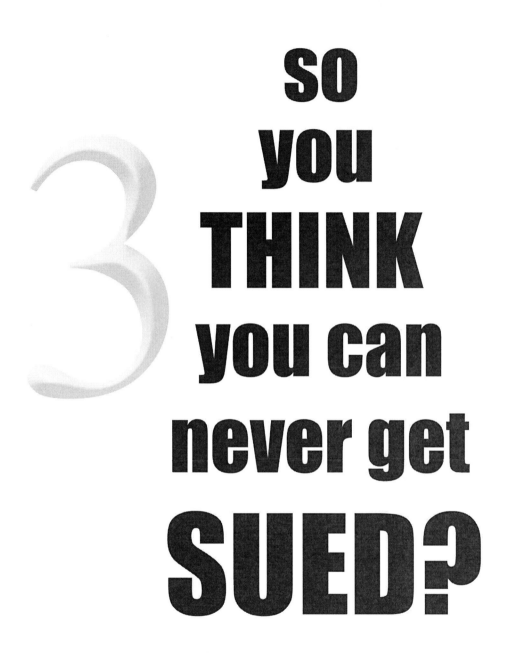

3

SO YOU THINK you can never get SUED?

Think again.

ohn is a third-generation member of his family's law firm. His grandfather opened up a now-prestigious, nationally-recognized Washington D.C. firm many years ago. It's New Year's Eve Day and as usual, John is excited about the prospect of the coming year—another banner year. Life is great!

About 9:30 a courier package arrives from another firm—an almost daily event and more good news, no doubt. Many of John's professional peers refer work to him and his firm. He opens the letter while sipping his coffee and glances at the first page. He frowns. Ruff & Oldmen are suing John's firm for a contractual error and omission. Then he chuckles. He's instituted strict workflows and guidelines for every single aspect of this file. Still. . .

The Research Begins

ohn calls in the two lawyers who worked on this case along with the paralegal who assisted them. He asks for copies of the file. What happened? Who did what and when? He calls in his two partners as this last day

37

of the year is a "half day blow-off day." They normally have a quick sandwich and even an adult beverage to celebrate another successful year gone by. Now they compare notes and scour the file. The room goes quiet. It seems that there has indeed been an error on the part of the two lawyers who worked on this case. The scary part is that it's a technical error to do with a statute of limitations on filings, an error frequently committed by lawyers without consequence. But Ruff & Oldmen are demanding $2,000,000. John sends the other lawyers out and turns his chair to look out the window at the city. "At least I'm covered by our insurance," he thinks. "At least we *think* I'm covered. I'd *better* be covered." He sits up. "I sure *hope* I'm covered," he says out loud.

John places a call to his insurance broker Lee, who of course is off until after the New Year and as luck would have it, New Year's Eve is on a weekend. He fumbles for ten minutes to contact the insurance company's 24-hour claims office. He finally gets hold of an adjuster who tells him to just "do your best" and "I'll call you on Monday." It will be three full days before John can talk to someone qualified.

The New Year. After three days of suspense, John finally talks to the adjuster who calmly informs him that he is, in fact, *not* covered for this particular incident. His lawyers' professional liability policy has a lot of fine print—lawyers are supposed to know about fine print—which is full of exclusions. He had no idea that 99 per cent of all such insurance policies have this particular exclusion. He and his two partners will now have to defend this case and face the possibility of having to pay the full demand of $2,000,000 on a technicality.

The sad ending is that they settled out of court for $600,000 with $200,000 having to come out of each partner's own pocket. Happy New Year! It didn't have to be that way.

You have an insurance policy. Now ask yourself: would you have known about this stated exclusion? Sure?

I THINK WE *MAY* HAVE A *SERIOUS ISSUE* HERE...

Growing the Practice

Evan owned a small firm with his brother Kenneth in Miami. They had a secretary/paralegal who was dynamite. Both brothers were well respected in the legal community for the way they practiced law. When a rival lawyer lost a case to them, the rival generally still felt good because both Evan and Kenneth were just plain nice gentlemen and fair and well-prepared lawyers.

Because they were so well liked, Evan and Kenneth were always being approached by peers wanting to join their firm. Somehow the timing never seemed right. But one day, they

were approached by Jack Ratzer, one of the area's top lawyers in their field of expertise. Jack wanted to retire early as he had made it big in real estate outside of his practice. The proposed merger made great sense because and Jack's specialized skills were well matched to their own and the timing was right.

A deal was made. As a part of the deal, Jack was made a partner in Evan's and Kenneth's firm for one year during the transition period. The idea was to ease his clients acceptance that the brothers were indeed at Jack's level and would offer representation that was in every way as satisfactory.

And what a year it was. Business was better than ever as the newly configured law firm doubled revenues. Life was indeed sweet. The brothers worked their tails off and earned every bit of their success Then, just shy of the one year mark, they received a certified letter that they were being sued for $500,000 for a client of Jack's who was being sued on a land deal where he felt Jack made an error in his advise of this client.

Like John, the brothers' thoughts turned to their insurance policy. Their lawyers professional liability insurance would cover this type of risk, right? They contacted the claims adjuster. To their shock and dismay, they learned that they had no coverage for this type. The exclusion that applied, known as "tail coverage" meant that although they had doubled their revenues, if judged against, they faced a substantial loss. In the end they settled at $350,000, of which they paid half up front. They subsequently got a bank loan to keep their cash flow in the black and ultimately their doors open.

Most lawyers and law firms are completely unaware that *one hundred per cent* of all insurance policies *do not have* coverage in cases such as John's and the brothers' disasters. A generalist insurance broker may have no awareness of such things, and anyway, a generalist can only offer policy holders what his or her company offers.

The thinking may be that such losses are unlikely to happen to ourselves or if they did, they're sort of inevitable. In other words, there's nothing you can do—just roll with the punches and take the hit. Neither thing is true.

The Specialist Knows the Insurance Companies

The legal insurance specialist knows and understands about such things, and not only is aware of how to add on such coverage so the client firm will be completely protected, but also knows exactly which insurance companies offers such add-ons.

Back to our medical comparisons. Again, heart surgeons. There may be hundreds of heart surgeons around the country, but the top surgeons work out of about five primary hospitals known for their premier heart surgeons. In the same way, as a law-firm insurance specialist, we're aware of each of the top insurance companies and the specialties that each one offers.

The surprise for most lawyers is that this kind of coverage is extremely affordable. The problem is not that such coverage is cost prohibitive; the problem is lack of knowledge and lack of awareness.

If you find you do not have this coverage, you are well within your rights to fire your generalist insurance broker. It's your livelihood at stake.

Leverage and Respect

When we become aware of these kinds of coverage needs, we go to the top insurance companies and bring it to their attention. Working as a liaison between insurers and customers, we suggest how they can better serve their policy holders. Top specialists have the leverage and the respect of the insurance

companies who can then write specific add-on products for that are tailored to lawyers and law firms. You will never have this kind of specialized service from an insurance generalist. Can you afford that kind of risk?

4 DATA Breach and Cyber Liability

Arguably Your Biggest Threat and Risk!

hat you are about to read should send shivers down your spine as **Cyber Liability and Data Breach** are the newest and most likely risk any office faces. Law Offices **especially** are at risk!

Not carrying Cyber Liability and Data Breach protection puts you at massive risk to lose everything you own including your reputation for something frankly that is out of your complete control.

Allow us to share a story about Robert who is now a client, yet wasn't prior. Robert is the Managing Partner of a very successful three Lawyer Firm with a tremendous support staff of four.

Robert's firm enjoys a reputation that is second to none and deservedly so as their marketing is outstanding, their procedures are as tight as a drum, and their technical understanding and practice of law within their area of practice makes them the "go to" Law Firm in the greater Dallas area for both clients and referring Lawyers.

And then "it" happened.

Robert received a call from one of the firm's clients claiming that they had suffered identity fraud.

At first Robert was baffled and frankly insulted that they'd blame him as his firm has state of the art firewalls protecting their computer system. So "how does this happen and why blame us" he thought?

Robert called an emergency meeting with the entire office and shared the nature of this very disturbing phone call. Immediately he saw a look of dismay on one of the other Lawyers David's face.

Robert being quick to read people thanked everyone for their time and closed the meeting. David went into Robert's office and reminded Robert that when he was traveling a few weeks prior he had lost his tablet or that it was stolen.

He remembered the inconvenience of David either losing or getting his tablet stolen and to get him back up and running was the focus (totally makes sense), yet never thought of a tablet as being a threat to any client's personal information. Robert knew right then and there that was the root cause of what was now a problem brewing.

So Robert called his insurance broker at the time who proceeded to share that he didn't know if this was covered or not, yet he'd get a claim filed and see what happens. Robert then asked correctly is there any type of protection for this type of risk of which his broker replied "I think so, yet let me check."

Of course two days later the claim was denied and Robert was dismayed as he had no idea how this would go from here. He did ask his insurance broker again if there was some sort of protection available for this and he answered "sort of yet it is very expensive and hard to get." Robert sarcastically replied "how comforting" and then hung up the phone.

Robert's client didn't suffer tremendous damage as they had an identity fraud service tip them off of this Data Breach and asked only that Robert's firm pay for the cost to repair their credit. All told this "only" cost Robert's Law Firm approximately $5,000.

Yet Robert thought that this could have been so much worse, and do you know what? Robert is spot on correct! He got to thinking that this may be the tip of the iceberg as who else may have been exposed as they have hundreds if not thousands of clients at risk as David had a VPN and internet connections to the office via that tablet.

Then he thought that anything is possible when it comes to client's information being compromised. From a hacker getting into his network or computer and capturing his clients' personal information. Understanding now more than ever that he and his firm are "toast" as it **will** get traced back.

And what about a laptop or even a smart phone, yet alone the tablet that David lost? In today's world, who doesn't own one of them, if not all three? And if you or any of your staff accidentally lose one of them or they are stolen you are again absolute "toast"!

Oh, and you'd be shocked at how many disgruntled employees who want to hurt you on their way out the door intentionally release confidential clients information as identity theft is big business in the world today that costs multiple billions annually in losses. You again are on the hook here and it doesn't have to be that way!

Almost every state has a law that makes it mandatory for every business that has suffered a Data Breach to notify every client that a potential Data Breach may have occurred to them and to check their credit and financial information.

Robert did his research and saw that his Law Firm could face up to $250,000 in fines in Texas if they did not notify every client of the potential Data Breach. So Robert and his entire staff had to spend nearly 60 hours combined to notify all clients of this breach via mail and email. Think of the time and money lost to his Law Firm doing this!

Oh and it gets better! Robert's letter caused more alarm than it did goodwill which caused many clients to leave Robert's Law Firm.

See, Cyber Liability and Data Breach protects you from any type of occurrence where your clients or employees personal information becomes compromised including third party damages and defense costs. Plus, it also will absolutely pay for the cost to mail all of your clients including the writing of the letter notifying your clients of a potential Data Breach to them so that it is well-received and comforting to your clients whereas the loss of clients leaving your firm will be minimal at worst if any at all. And yes, all done and paid by your insurance company who specializes in this type of claim day in and day out!

And am going to again restate how any of this can easily happen to you that could frankly ruin you.

Your computers at work being hacked.

Or a disgruntled employee taking clients or employees information.

A laptop, tablet, smart phone lost or stolen.

Specifically, Data Breach & Cyber Liability is for Law Offices because you certainly collect personal information from your clients as highlights of the protection provided include:

♦ Third party defense and damages protection
♦ Comprehensive breach response solution including forensic, legal, notification, credit and identity monitoring, call center, and public relations services
♦ Notification provided on a number of affected individuals basis to persons who must be notified under applicable

law or those who are determined to be subject to risk of financial, reputational or other harm.

♦ Forensic and legal assistance from a panel of experts to help determine the extent of the breach and the steps needed to comply with applicable privacy laws

♦ Each notified individual to receive an offer for 12 months of free 3-bureau credit monitoring or identity monitoring

♦ Identity theft-related fraud resolution services for individuals enrolled in credit monitoring who become victims of identity theft

♦ Coverage for website content media liability (offline media coverage is also available)

Yes, this is all covered for you if you purchase Data Breach and Cyber Liability.

<u>**And AGAIN here is a key point:**</u> Most every state requires companies to notify customers if there is a Data Breach. If you don't, you are subject to huge fine and disciplinary action.

Don't fool yourself either, as hackers and cybercriminals are very opportunistic. If they can get 100 records from a Law Firm they'll do it.

And it gets worse as there is an increase in the number of customers the firms surveyed lost after a Data Breach. It's no surprise for those who are not protected with Data Breach insurance lost on average 18 percent of their clients as bad news travels very quickly!

The risk of not having Data Breach and Cyber Liability insurance protection is pennies on the dollar as compared to the massive loss you will suffer if you do not have this valuable protection.

income &
OUTCOME

expecting the
unexpected

Dan is the founder and managing general partner of a well-respected firm in Atlanta. It is *the* go-to law firm for personal injury cases because of Dan's great marketing and success trying cases on behalf of plaintiffs.

One spring, however, a tornado rips through that area and blows Dan's premises to the ground. It happened in the late evening and thankfully no one is hurt. Dan places a call to his agent, confident that everything is covered. It's a tornado, for heaven's sake.

Dan is especially concerned about his three great paralegals, and his star office manager whom he desperately wants to keep. The trusted employees are asking him, "What are we going to do? We know we can't work while you're rebuilding. That's going to take several months."

Dan's sure there is coverage for that. It only makes sense! Gene, Dan's genial generalist insurance broker, calls him two days after the disaster. He seems nervous. He tells Dan that he'll need to see all the paperwork. Dan is incredulous. His "paperwork" is probably at that moment scattered across a

muddy field in the next county. Gene informs Dan that it seems he has limited protection for this situation, so "you'd better tell your employees to get jobs elsewhere." Then he adds "But I'm sure they'll come back to you when you're ready."

When, several months later, Dan once again opens his doors, his three great employees have taken new jobs with a rival firm and don't really want to job-jump. Within a year, Dan has to close his doors because he can never fully recuperate from this catastrophe. He joins this same rival firm. They tell him he'll have to earn partner status. He enjoyed 27 years as a superstar lawyer and this is where he ends up?

Had he had the proper protection, he could have either opened up a temporary location, or even retained his loyal key employees without missing a beat.

It Doesn't Have to Be That Way

This is a sad story that happens time and time again. We hear these stories all the time in our work. It doesn't have to be that way. Sometimes lawyers will tell us they were able to "get a great deal" with their insurance. They truly believe they're saving money. The truth is they are putting their entire livelihood at risk. We watch as they go under and lose everything simply because their "great deal" did not give them the protection they needed—for no reason but lack of specialized knowledge on everyone's part. How could lawyers, who are often specialists themselves, overlook that?

Actual Loss Sustained

If your business is shut down due to any type of calamity, even a generalist insurance broker should have you covered in what is called an "actual loss sustained" up to twelve months. This means whatever losses are

DO YOU MEAN THAT *MY* INCOME IS *LIMITED,* OR NOT EVEN COVERED?

incurred—lost revenue, profits, salaries to retain key employees—all are of your business is shut down due to any type of calamity, even a generalist insurance broker should have you covered in what is called an "actual loss sustained" up to twelve months. This means whatever losses are incurred—lost revenue, profits, salaries to retain key employees—all are covered. This can refer to the tornado described in the preceding pages or fire or similar catastrophes.

Half of all policies are written on a "guestimate" rate. They *guess* how much your revenues are. In our opinion, this

is one of the most miswritten, improperly placed types of protection on any insurance policy.

This is a very tricky area. It pertains to policies for any and all types of businesses, ranging from law firms to the local transmission shop. The same problems prevail.

"Actual loss sustained," does not put a limit on the loss. If your revenues were $20,000 a week and you are shut down for twelve weeks, you will receive the equivalent of $240,000. You don't have to deal with *proving* it or working with any formulas.

Calculating the Loss

I f as the founder or managing general partner of your firm, you also own the building, those mortgage payments will not stop just because a tornado flattens your place of business. Likewise, if you lease the building, the lease payments do not stop. Compensation for these kinds of expenses must be included in the loss.

This type of coverage allows for the opening of a temporary location until the present location is repaired and restored. This is crucial, because the other possible loss in a catastrophic situation is the loss of regular clients. You don't want those clients to start doing business with all your competitors. Everything that can be done must be done to retain customers. Otherwise, as in Dan's case, the business may go under for good.

Our message here is that you can protect your profits, your regular expenses, retain key employees, and retain loyal clients as well.

If you have a great office manager or a great paralegal—or many of both—you ask them to sign an agreement that they will not moonlight or go to a competitor's to work. No *double-dipping*. They will then receive their full income for the length of time that it takes for the business to be up and running again. Those key employees can have an extended vacation and still get paid.

The Waiting Time

Again, when talking about being covered for a loss of business income, the waiting time must be brought into the equation. Few generalist insurance brokers even think about how crucial this is to law firms.

In other words, even if your policy has the "actual loss sustained" clause included, it may be diluted by an extended waiting period. The insurance companies that write proper policies for law firms will provide an add-on that takes the time waiting period down to zero.

Let's say the disaster is an electrical fire within the building and it must close down for four days. This is not as catastrophic as being leveled by a tornado, but can still amount to a sizeable loss. On most policies law firms will lose at least the first full day's revenue if not the first three days. That, in essence, is like having no coverage at all. It's useless. If the waiting time is 72 hours and the firm is shut down for four days, the partners really only have 25% protection. Is that what you want for your practice?

This is why it's so crucial to have a zero waiting period clearly stated in the policy. That way, if you lose four days, you will be compensated for the entire time.

Miswritten and Messed Up!

As we said previously, this is without a doubt the most miswritten and *messed up* portion of any law firm insurance policy. This is because it's handled by a generalist insurance broker who has little or no comprehension of the particular needs of this specialized insurance business. Yesterday that insurance broker was

working with the flower shop down the street; the day before it was with a car dealership. Nothing wrong with that, except for the fact that that insurance broker simply is not well versed about your specific needs as lawyers.

This lack of knowledge on the part of your insurance broker can actually mean the difference between your firm surviving a catastrophic event or going down and going under—permanently. It's no small matter.

Run Fast!

If you do not have a policy that includes "actual loss sustained," this is your first clue to run and run fast! Get this policy replaced as fast as you possibly can. Every minute you delay is another minute that you are tempting fate. The chances that this pertains to your policy are very large. We've found that less than 50% of the policies out there even have "actual loss sustained" included. And even with these, a *zero wait period is never included*.

For the lawyers and law firms insurance specialist, this is no problem at all. It's like asking mom for another piece of apple pie. We ask for these add-ons because we know they are vital to the very survival of our client's livelihood. And our longstanding relationship with the companies we deal with assures us the answer will be *yes*. Most insurance brokers don't even think in these terms.

When you have a legal firm insurance specialist on your side, you can go run your practice, do what you do best and stop spending your time worrying. You truly are covered. You can sleep peacefully at night. When Mother Nature whips up a storm, or when bad luck hits your place with a fire, when an unfortunate accident occurs, when you have a dishonest employee, you will still have a smile on your face, because you *know* you have the right kind of protection.

6

running
ERRANDS

to ruination

rin's law firm is located in the Dallas/Fort Worth area. Erin, the oldest of four girls, daughters of a prominent Texas lawyer, has marketed her firm as family-friendly to groups who live in the vicinity. She is known personally for her local charity work and is well liked and respected in the community.

Being a busy firm, the staff often runs out of simple office supplies or needs to get packages delivered to the court house or another firm or even a client. This may happen many times every week.

The Infamous Accident

ne early January day, Erin sent her office manager Mitch to the courthouse since he was going to an early dinner at his sister's nearby barbeque restaurant. It was the one day a month that the three partners and Mitch could go over the firm's business. The setting sun was glaring in his eyes and Mitch, who was driving

his own car and keeping to the speed limit, didn't see the car stopping in front of him and had a rear end collision.

Mitch knew he had great car insurance and he didn't have undue concern about the matter. However the driver of the other car, named Craig, had years earlier sustained sports injuries to his back and neck. At the time of the accident, Craig was the head basketball coach at the local university and pulling down a sizeable income.

The impact of this rear-ending incident exacerbated the existing injuries to the point that Craig would no longer be able to fulfill his coaching duties and therefore sustained a loss of income. With two years remaining on his coaching contract, he could very closely estimate the amount of the loss that he would be incurred when the university released him from the contract—which they subsequently did.

Where Will the Money Come From?

Mitch's personal auto insurance coverage allowed for $300,000 in damages. Where would the rest of the over one million dollars come from? We're sure you've already guessed the answer. A good personal injury attorney quickly discovered that Mitch was running an errand for Erin's legal firm on business time.

Under deposition Mitch was certainly not going to lie. Nor would he ever think he needed to. He would clearly state that he was on an errand for his boss. Now that attorney knew that Mitch was on business time, so he went after Erin's firm. Erin was certain she was protected. After all, she had general liability. Then she learned the frightening truth: general liability is only for your premises! And this was definitely *not* on the premises.

Chapter 6

MY *PERSONAL* CAR INSURANCE IS *ENOUGH* . . . *I HOPE!*

What Was Missing?

What did Erin need that she did not have? It's called "Hired Non-Owned Auto Coverage." This coverage costs a little over $100 per year for a million dollars' worth of protection. Because Erin didn't have this coverage, she would have a lien against her property and be sued for all her profits and maybe be put out of business.

While this turned out to be a multi-million lawsuit, we know that if Erin had had the correct coverage, Craig and his

attorney would have taken the million offered and gone their way. We've seen it happen. They were looking for the easy way out, and proper coverage provides it.

A lawyer reading this may think this story doesn't apply in his or her case since they never run out of any supplies or never send an employee anywhere. It doesn't necessarily have to be an errand to pick up items; it could happen during the daily bank run. Any personal injury lawyer worth his salt will learn this was a business errand on business time, and therefore they will go where the money is. They will sue the business itself.

Even though this sort of liability arises from a legal matter, the majority of law firms we see do not have the proper coverage. Since they are not involved in deliveries, they don't see the need. But for the price, it's just not worth the risk. Why leave yourself wide open for such a disastrous lawsuit?

7

FLOODS
earthquakes
harassment
discrimination
TERMINATION

the grisly gremlins of
EXCLUSION

hether you believe in global warming or not, it sure seems as if the weather patterns in the United States have become more and more severe since the turn of the century and there are certainly parts of the nation that are in harm's way when it comes to floods and earthquakes. Lenders normally require businesses in those areas to purchase protection against these catastrophic events. It's also common sense.

Now understand that both flood and earthquake protection is 100% excluded by all insurance companies. That's why it's worth talking about this right here, right now before it is too late. The alternative might be your personal and business ruination.

Look at the catastrophic week of August 22, 2011, when Washington D.C. and Philadelphia—to name just two major metropolitan areas—experienced earthquake damage. Damage to businesses totaled approximately $15 million dollars but it's been estimated that less than 1% of all businesses

in those cities had any type of earthquake protection. The extremely sad part of this is that the average cost nationally to insure for earthquake protection is in the hundreds of dollars range at most. At Insuring Lawyer, earthquake is always endorsed on all policies to protect you properly. Your current generalist insurance broker is snoozing at your peril. Fire him or her right now and get protected properly!

The Last Week of August 2011

As if the earthquake that rocked Washington DC and Philadelphia on August 23, 2011 wasn't enough, Hurricane Irene came blowing through that weekend causing unprecedented flooding to the eastern seaboard, literally wiping out entire communities.

The killer factor was that areas hundreds of miles inland and not designated as flood plains sustained catastrophic flooding. Early estimates were that only 20% of these businesses in those areas had flood protection. This was a potential death blow to many of them.

Once again the shocking and sad part is that if your firm is not in a flood plain, the cost to protect your practice is highly affordable, usually running around $1,000 annually. It only makes sense to budget less than $3 day to protect your livelihood from being wiped out. And don't think you can keep an eye on the Weather Channel and purchase flood protection a week or a few days ahead of time because there is always a 30-day waiting period.

Act today and make it fit your budget—or risk Mother Nature being the ultimate decider of your fate.

THIS *CANNOT* BE *HAPPENING!* WE AREN'T EVEN IN A *FLOOD ZONE!*

Harassment, Discrimination and Unfair Termination

Harassment, discrimination and unfair termination lawsuits are swarming in our present society. Since frivolous lawsuits abound, it only makes sense to understand this area of business and be prepared.

Sad to say, this is a policy that only about 5% of lawyers and law firms choose to purchase. The average cost runs from $800 to $1500 annually. This means you're looking at about $5 per day.

What does such protection cover and why is it needed? Examples of harassment vary and are often nothing like what the average person imagines.

Not What You Imagine

In a certain legal firm, a male lawyer took a liking to one of the paralegals with whom he worked. His motives were innocent. He didn't feel he was harassing her. He truly liked her. While he was not being aggressive, he was persistent. Because of that, the paralegal, who did not share his feelings, finally got fed up with his pursuit and quit. She then filed a suit stating that she was forced to quit because she was being *harassed*. If that firm in question doesn't have the right protection, they will be out the defense cost. The average defense cost for any harassment, discrimination and termination lawsuit is $58,000. Are you surprised? Most lawyers we talk to have no idea it could be that expensive just to prove their innocence.

The foregoing example is between non-partners, but let's looks at another situation.

Owner and Employee

Martin is the managing general partner of a third generation well-known and respected law firm situated in the suburbs of Detroit. Martin worked hard and had done so all his life. He'd bent over backward to make his practice known as the go-to player for estate planning. People from all over Michigan made it a point to consult his firm for their estate planning needs.

Martin was a former All Big Ten linebacker who'd played three years professionally and used language that would be considered a bit spicy. While he would never take the Lord's name in vain, he did use a wide variety of the other types of off-color language. When things didn't go exactly right, Martin also had a touch of bad temper. People who knew him shared that this was nothing more than his testosterone kicking in and one of his strengths. That was especially when the spicy language would come forth. However, he was careful that it only happened when he was in his office—never within earshot of clients.

One young secretary, unbeknownst to Martin, took great offense at this and to his surprise Martin was presented with a lawsuit for using foul language. He was especially surprised because neither his anger, nor his foul language, had ever been directed toward this particular secretary or anyone associated in his firm. He was quickly to learn that that did not matter. He still had a lawsuit with which to deal!

Interviewees

Unsuspecting lawyers find themselves in a real dilemma due to a segment of society who are professionals at filing lawsuits over hiring discrimination. These people are looking for a quick five to ten thousand dollars and will proceed to accuse a business of not hiring because they are the wrong color, wrong size, and wrong age and so on.

Granted there are some such lawsuits that are legitimate, but the point is in our over-zealous, litigious society, it can happen to any firm at any time. It will take a minimum of forty hours of attorney time to get rid of the insidious thing and that could take at the least ten grand out of pocket.

Clients

The hidden gremlin of harassment can also pop out in the form of a client. In one case it was at Nate's firm in Denver, known locally and even nationally as a great place for professional athletes and entertainers

THE *CLIENT* IS *ALWAYS* RIGHT . . . *RIGHT?. . .WRONG!*

to get the best representation. One big superstar was getting a little overly zealous in his flirting with the one of the paralegals. Since it was somewhat out of character for this particular client, Nate tended to overlook it and quite honestly thought the paralegal (the one who had the courage to complain) was being overly sensitive.

She ended up quitting her job and filed a harassment suit against Nate's firm. She had been with Nate for a number of years and this was her main job, but she was simply unable to handle this situation.

At first Nate was incredulous, thinking the suit was against him. Then he learned it was due to the prominent client. Other support staff were then subpoenaed and under deposition had to tell the truth about the matter. They had to relate that this particular client had been acting inappropriately.

Nate quickly learned that he had no coverage at all for such things. He settled out of court for $100,000. The paralegal got her job back, and the court ordered that the wealthy client be banned from any contact with her—naturally humiliating for *him*. The entire situation was bad for everyone involved.

Discrimination

In a well-respected firm in St. Louis, a junior Lawyer felt that an African American couple was being exceptionally demanding of him. He seemed unable to please them. Finally, becoming exasperated, as he turned away he made a derogatory remark. He thought they couldn't hear, but not only did they hear, others nearby heard it as well.

The partners of this particular firm ended up settling out of court for $75,000. But that wasn't the end of it. They also ended up paying another $35,000 in legal fees. Their firm was required to set up training for all staff and partners (they had several locations), which cost an additional $10,000. And it hit the newspapers, which was publicity of the worst sort.

Gray Areas

There are so many gray areas within harassment and discrimination complaints, it's hard to even guess what might happen. No one lawyer can be everywhere at once. Whether you have one location or ten, things will happen that are totally out of your control.

Every legal firm likes to think that they are fair and equitable in all their dealings with staff and clients. While that may be true, as we've seen in these examples, many circumstances are beyond the partners' control. It is so much more than what you as the managing general partner do or do not do in your day-to-day running of your practice.

This is why, in our opinion, this is coverage lawyers cannot afford to be without. Employment Practices Liability Insurance (EPLI, as it is called) is far-reaching and even takes in the almost unimaginable—as in the examples we've seen here appeared to the lawyers involved. This type of protection would cost anywhere from $800 – $1,500 annually.

Added Benefit

As a service to all our clients, we have an easy-to-read handbook that details for lawyers and law firms how to train their staff to avert these types of problems before they happen.

This is just one of many added benefits we make available for all our clients to help them build and maintain a successful practice.

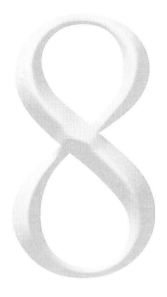

more than hurt
FEELINGS

orkers Compensation is truly the easiest and most straightforward coverage contract to write for any insurance broker.

What Is Workers' Compensation Insurance?

Workers' Compensation insurance, sometimes called Workman's Compensation insurance, Workers' Liability insurance, or Workers' Comp insurance covers your employees' medical expenses and at least some portion of their lost wages if they are injured on the job.

How Does Workers' Compensation Insurance Protect Your Business?

Most states require companies to purchase workers' compensation insurance for their employees. Four states (Ohio, Washington, North Dakota, and Wyoming) have "pools" of insurance that are available for you to purchase, but in most states, companies must find private workers' compensation policies. Because workers' comp insurance is mandated by law, lawyers often think that it is just one more overhead expense that provides little benefit. But good workers' compensation insurance is actually an affordable benefit that protects both you and your employees.

Following are the optional parts of Workers' Comp insurance policies that have an impact on the cost and value of the coverage for you and your employees:

In the employers' liability section, or "part two" coverage, your legal expenses would be covered if an employee makes an inappropriate claim of work-related illnesses or injuries. While this section is almost always included in workman's compensation insurance, you can choose the amount of liability coverage in this section.

- Coverage for employees who are injured in states outside those where your business normally operates.
- Coverage for various types of injuries and illnesses. The mandated part of this section depends on the state where your business is located, but you should be aware of what is and is not covered.
- Coverage for funeral expenses and financial support to dependents.
- Reimbursement percentages for lost wages.

The cost of workers' comp insurance can vary widely depending on these options, so if you are comparing premium costs, you need to be aware of these variables.

Chapter 8

OUCH! OUCH!

Workers' Compensation Rules

There are websites designed to address your own state's insurance regarding worker's compensation insurance rules and requirements.

Where the Generalist Insurance Broker Can Hurt You in Your Wallet

Because Workers Comp coverage is very straightforward, as a lawyer your risk is not in being properly protected, but being charged the incorrect premium.

This Mistake Is So Common That It Hurts To Even Write About It

We will share numerous "insider secrets" so that you keep your hard earned money where it belongs, not wasted on overcharging Workers Comp insurance premiums from either an apathetic or incompetent insurance broker.

Make 100% certain that your reports of payroll premium per class of employee are accurate. In other words, do not assume paralegals are a lower rate than a junior lawyer, etc. An expert in law firms will know this.

Make sure that when an employee suffers injury that the correct reserve is placed and that the claim gets settled quickly. This keeps your rating modification low—meaning you pay less in premiums.

Always make sure you have in place the very safest conditions for your employees. This will allow your rate to go down every year at renewal.

These are so simple yet it is estimated that 78% of all lawyers and law firms have their Workers Compensation written improperly, costing them on average $1,700 annually. This is real money and you can correct the situation today with one simple call to us.

The key to getting the best insurance coverage, specific for the legal field, is to retain an insurance broker who not only specializes in law practices but also is a fellow business owner. You don't want an insurance company employee as your insurance broker. You want someone who's going to work for *you*, not someone whose paycheck is tied to one company. You need an insurance broker who can shop the market, compare prices, and get the most comprehensive coverage for you— maybe even use multiple companies for your total coverage.

You want a good price? And you want ultimate protection when disaster strikes? Use an independent insurance broker who specializes in insurance for the legal profession and who owns his own business.

9

LAWYERS
professional
liability

*How to easily plug
all fatal gaps
to leverage the multi-billion
dollar insurance industry
to your advantage*

Too often the enemy of being great is simply being good versus being awful. In fact, if something is perceived to be good or good enough then it is often deemed acceptable. Yet by reading our book, our feeling is that you are a person that does not settle for the status quo.

See in our litigious society, too many excellent law firms have had allegations of malpractice made against them. Professional liability insurance policy form language is critically important. It can mean the difference between whether your insurance company will pay claims that may result.

You need to know that not all Lawyers Professional Liability (LPL) insurance policies are created equally, and even if the policy under consideration does not contain the policy language and coverage that you desire, you can negotiate the coverage that you need, sometimes at little to even no additional cost.

Optional Endorsements—Your Key to Great Coverage

L et's begin with the understanding that the main body of a policy form is what is called a "filed form," meaning that it has been approved by your home states Department of Insurance, therefore it cannot be changed in the same manner as say a contract between two private parties. Yet it still can be amended through endorsements.

These endorsements are also known as "filed forms". Your home states Department of Insurance will recognize that one policy form does not fit every situation, so they allow insurers to use these endorsements to tailor specific coverage that meets the needs of your individual law firm.

These endorsements are called "optional endorsements," meaning that they are attached to the main policy form, and they change the coverage offered under the main policy form by your insurer. Some optional endorsements expand coverage while others take coverage away.

By now am sure you are saying to yourself, "Why would our states Department of Insurance allow an insurer to take away coverage through an optional endorsement?" Because in some cases, an insurer will only offer terms to a law firm if it carves out exceptions to coverage in a particular area of concern. Otherwise, the insurance company's only other option would be to decline to offer coverage to your firm at all. Optional endorsements are structured much as would be amendments to a contract between two private parties. For example, language such as, "Section I. INSURING AGREEMENT, paragraph A. is hereby amended with the following. . . ."

If for example your law firm read paragraph A of the "Insuring Agreement" of the main policy form of your LPL insurance and understood it that you're covered, but did not read the optional endorsement that took away coverage, then your firm could be without some if not all coverage you initially understood to have when a claim arises.

Therefore it is absolutely a must regarding optional endorsements for you to review the language contained not only in the main policy form of your LPL policy, but also in each optional endorsement offered. And here is where it gets very tricky and having a specialist with LPL will make all of the difference in the world. See these endorsements can be identified by the title and form number of each optional endorsement to include as part of a policy in your quotes to the insurance broker, but they usually do not include the actual endorsements themselves.

The titles of the optional endorsements can give you clues about their content, but these titles are usually not very descriptive. The better, more sophisticated insurance brokers will ask to review the language in these optional endorsements before presenting quotes to you. However, the ultimate responsibility for reviewing policy form language, including

all optional endorsements, belongs to you. Yet wouldn't it only make sense that an expert in LPL would be best suited to identify any fatal gaps in your protection up front?

You Must Know What to Ask For

As would be the case in any negotiation, you need to define up front what is important for your Law Firm. While lawyers are trained to review their client's contracts in everyday practice, it never ceases to amaze us how often law firms don't read their very own LPL policies.

Why is that? It would be our opinion over the years to surmise that lawyers just do not know that their policy form is indeed negotiable, so they pretty much review the "policy highlights" quote or analysis sheet comparing coverage between what they have and what is being offered.

This is serious business here folks as what is accepted by you is extremely meaningful in claims scenarios, and it frankly does not take long to determine whether your policy provides what coverage you have, need, and don't have. In fact, a true LPL expert will identify by your practice what are your exposures and provide you with this information. If not, you should fire that insurance broker immediately.

In fact, in the next section we'll describe examples of important coverage options that you should try to negotiate on behalf of your firm, and whether these coverage enhancements are typically available for free or with an approximate additional premium charge.

Mutual Choice of Counsel—Who Is Going to Defend You?

 ost LPL insurance companies do not offer "mutual choice of counsel" coverage in their standard policies. The reason is that an insurer's claim department wants to maintain as much control over the claims adjustment process as possible. The claims department typically sets up a list of "panel counsel" that handles its LPL claims that occur within a certain geographic area.

For example, if your insurer receives a malpractice claim for you then they will typically assign the defense of that claim to one of the law firms on its "panel counsel" list for your home state. These "panel counsel" firms have agreed to abide by the insurer's litigation guidelines and to the insurer's hourly rates. These firms also must have demonstrated experience defending lawyers against malpractice claims. So far, so good.

While these "panel counsel" firms *should* defend your firm competently in the event of a claim, your firm may wish to participate in selecting a law firm. In some cases, you may desire to select a firm that is not on a carrier's list of "panel counsel."

This is where if you have "mutual choice of counsel" coverage endorsed onto your policy if it wasn't included (which most will not include it automatically), then both you and your insurer come to an agreement about which law firm will defend your firm in your claim. If you suggest a law firm that is not on your insurers "panel counsel" list, then that firm you suggested will need to agree to your insurer's litigation management guidelines and rates. Of course, your suggested law firm will also need to demonstrate expertise in defending legal malpractice claims. In rare cases where your firm and your insurer cannot agree on a law firm to defend your firm against a malpractice claim, then your insurer will select a defense firm on its own.

While this coverage is very rarely offered in the main policy form of most insurers, it usually can be added as an optional endorsement. Typically, if your insurer agrees to add this endorsement to its policy, it will do so for no additional premium. Yet do realize that your insurer most likely will resist adding this endorsement because they desire to retain control of their panel of defense counsel.

Deductibles—Very Much The Difference Maker

Almost all LPL insurance include a policy deductible. Typically, insurers seek deductibles in the range of $2,500 or more per attorney in a firm. Deductibles also vary by the liability coverage limits sought by law firms. If your law firm is willing to accept a larger deductible, only then will a carrier offer to provide higher liability coverage limits. For example, if your firm desires a $5 million limit, rarely will your insurer allow for a deductible of less than $10,000.

Since a deductible is incurred first in any claims scenario, it has an immediate impact on your firm's finances in the event of a claim. Yet there are many optional endorsements available that lessen the negative impact of a deductible on your law firm. Some of these optional endorsements are offered for additional premiums, and others are offered for free as you'll read about in the next section.

Aggregate Deductible—Stop the Hemorrhaging

Most insurers offer "aggregate deductibles." Most LPL policies are written with a "per claim" deductible, meaning that the deductible will apply to each and every claim experienced by your law firm in the policy year.

Since claims are relatively rare, per claim deductibles are satisfactory for most claims scenarios. However, sometimes situations will arise were your firm could experience what is known as "serial claims" as the result of some error that is usually a technicality which will have impact across a large volume of clients.

For example, if your law firm has an employee that has been engaging in collection activities against a large volume of debtors on behalf of one of your clients and your employee's practices violated the federal Fair Debt Collection Practices Act, or its state equivalent, then a separate deductible would apply to each claim against the firm.

So if your deductible was $2,500 per claim, and the damages claimed by each third party amounted to $2,000 then your insurer would not pay any damages because a separate $2,500 deductible would apply to each and every claim, even if there were hundreds of claims against your firm amounting to hundreds of thousands of dollars lost by your firm. NOT GOOD! Yet, aggregate deductibles are particularly important to your law firm as who wants to pay a large number of deductibles within the same policy year? Of course your law firm can pay your selected deductible and is why you chose it, but if your firm experienced five claims in a given year, would it pay five times your annual deductible?

So make certain that you have an aggregate deductible per claim endorsed onto your LPL policy which is usually done at a nominal charge.

Loss Only Deductibles—Pay Only If You Are Liable

Most insurers also offer "loss only deductibles," also known as "first-dollar defense" coverage. As the name implies, a law firm's deductible only applies if you are found to be negligent and a claim is made by your insurer on behalf of your firm. And the best part is that your deductible does not apply to defense costs. This coverage is attractive because defense costs are the first costs that your law firm incurs in a claim, and with meritless claims, usually law firms incur only defense costs.

This optional endorsement is available for an additional premium, but it is also subject to your insurers underwriting standards. If your firm and its area of expertise in your practice has shown a propensity for facing a large number of small claims or incidents, most likely your insurer will

decline to offer you this option. In other words, the underwriter may determine that the additional premium that they will incur will not likely offset the costs that they will incur by defending your firm from the first dollar.

The amount of additional premiums for both the "loss only deductible" and the "aggregate deductible" optional endorsements varies by the size of the deductible. Also, each insurer has its own unique pricing structure for these options. It is recommended to get alternate quotes for these options so that you may make the best decision for your firm.

Deductibles and Coverage Enhancements—The Fine Print Means Big Dollars

Over the years, several coverage features that were added to LPL policies to make them more competitive have been gradually adopted into most insurers policy forms. However, while some insurers have added these enhancements, they have not made corresponding changes to how their deductible for these enhancements work.

In other words, if a policy deductible still applies to these enhancements, then their value is greatly diminished. It is not always apparent if the deductible applies to these coverage enhancements or not. Here is a brief overview of some of these coverage enhancements.

Loss of Earnings Coverage—Yes, Your Time is Valuable

Many insurers nowadays include "loss of earnings" coverage in their LPL policies meaning this coverage reimburses you for lost wages while attending a deposition, trial, or other work time lost by you related to investigating or defending a claim on the request of the insurer.

Usually, there are caps to this enhanced coverage on a per day, per claim, and per policy period basis. For example, an insurer may offer up to $500 per insured per day for your time spent cooperating with your insurer to defend the claim, subject to a limit of $10,000 per claim and $50,000 per policy period for all insured attorneys in your firm. This coverage is usually provided with no additional premium.

So let's look at an example. Say your firm carries a $5,000 deductible, and it applies to this coverage enhancement at $500 per day, then your firm would have to incur at least 10 days' worth of lost wages before this coverage would come into effect. Clearly, the deductible in this situation would render the coverage enhancement much less advantageous to the firm, so you should investigate how the "loss of earnings" coverage interacts with your policy's deductible.

Disciplinary Proceedings—Complaints That Will Crush Your Cash Flow

Another common LPL policy coverage enhancement will pay for the cost of defending you in a proceeding that is brought by a disciplinary board that alleges professional misconduct. Insurers providing this coverage enhancement will pay for the costs of defending you up to a certain limit for each proceeding and an aggregate limit for all such proceedings in a given policy year.

For example, your insurer may provide $10,000 of defense costs per disciplinary proceeding and up to $25,000 per policy period. As with the "loss of earnings coverage," this coverage enhancement is usually provided with no additional premium. However, if your firm's deductible applies to this coverage, then a large portion of the benefit is eliminated.

Pro Bono Services—No Good Deed Goes Unpunished?

One relatively new coverage enhancement eliminates application of your firm's deductible to any legal services rendered by your firm to pro bono clients. If your law firm engages in pro bono services then you will be viewed positively by your insurer because it demonstrates a commitment by your firm to "doing the right thing" rather than on functioning solely as all about the money. If your firm is solely focused on making money, that might signal that you may, for example, cut expenses to the detriment of prudent risk management.

Wouldn't it be a shame if your firm had the out-of-pocket expense of the amount of a deductible if a pro bono client turned around and sued your firm for legal malpractice? Obviously, the larger your deductible the more valuable is this coverage.

It is not a common optional endorsement, but it is worth asking about. It is usually offered for no additional premium.

Professional Services—Beyond Being a "Lawyer"

Most LPL policies very expansively define "covered professional services" under the policies. These covered professional services typically include services rendered as a lawyer, arbitrator, mediator, notary public, executor, or trustee, for example. However, sometimes attorneys in your firm perform professional services on behalf of clients that do not meet these definitions.

Examples include acting in the capacity of a lobbyist, a member of the board of a bar association, an author of legal articles, or a speaker at legal conferences. Less common additions to a definition of covered professional services under a policy include services rendered as an expert witness or claims adjustment services.

If one of your attorneys commits malpractice in one of these capacities, and it is not included in your policy's definition of covered professional services, then the insurer might have the right to deny the claim.

It is often difficult to determine when an attorney takes his or her "lawyer hat" off and puts on his or her "lobbyist hat" instead. Nonetheless, to avoid ambiguity, it is best to evaluate your firm's professional services thoroughly, and make sure that your policy provides the coverage that you need.

Most insurers are able to expand the definition of covered professional services through the use of an optional endorsement, and usually without charging an additional premium. However, you will not get this coverage unless you ask for it! Also, as a side note, your insurer will not add professional services that are not typically performed by law firms. For instance, they will not add "accounting services" to its LPL policy definition of covered professional services. In that example, you would need to purchase a separate "accountants professional liability" policy to cover that exposure.

Exclusions—They Giveth And They Taketh Away

LPL insurance policies are written to cover pretty much anything that a lawyer does in his or her professional capacity for his or her clients, unless otherwise excluded under the policy.

Therefore, reviewing the exclusions in an LPL policy is critically important. Once again, it would be incorrect to assume that an insurers exclusions are not negotiable. Insurers often do have optional endorsements that modify or even eliminate exclusions that are in a policy. However, it is usually much more difficult to have these taken out.

First, an insurer will not eliminate exclusions that are considered essential to the nature of the LPL policy. For example, an insurer will not agree to remove the "bodily injury"

exclusion because that would have the effect of converting the LPL policy into a general liability policy.

An insurer also would not agree to eliminate the "intentional bad acts" exclusion because a properly drafted insurance policy would not cover intentionally fraudulent or criminal behavior. However, if there is a particular exclusion that would provide incomplete coverage to your law firm, then it would be wise to at least ask your insurer if it could remove the exclusion.

For example, some LPL policies exclude any securities work performed by a law firm because of the severity potential of such claims. If your firm does not perform traditional securities work by representing public companies in connection with their reporting obligations to the SEC, or engaging in private placements or municipal bond work, then you may think that such an exclusion is not meaningful.

However, some securities exclusions are written so broadly that even a simple incorporation of your client's business could be an excluded professional service under your policy. Therefore, it is very wise to evaluate all exclusions in your policy in light of your firm's particular practice.

Ownership in Clients—A Conflict of Interest?

L PL policies commonly eliminate coverage for professional services rendered to an entity that is owned by firm attorneys. One of the reasons for this exclusion is to eliminate the potential conflict of interest in those situations. For example, if an attorney owns 50 percent of a PL policies commonly eliminate coverage for professional services rendered to an entity that is owned by firm attorneys. One of the reasons for this exclusion is to eliminate the potential conflict of interest in those situations. For example, if an attorney owns 50 percent of a client of the attorney's firm, then it would be possible for that attorney to have his or her company sue his or her law firm and collect proceeds from the insurance company if the firm's LPL policy did not exclude "ownership in clients."

To avoid this potential conflict of interest, LPL policies typically exclude coverage for professional services rendered to a client whose stock is more than 10 percent or 15 percent owned by any attorney in the law firm. The actual ownership percentage cutoff varies among LPL insurers.

Nonetheless, many insurers have optional endorsements in place that can increase the ownership percentage that is used for your particular law firm's policy. Thus, if your firm has one client that is 25 percent owned by lawyers in the firm, it would be possible to obtain an endorsement that would cover that client under the law firm's LPL policy.

It may be possible to negotiate an ownership percentage as high as 35 percent from an insurer, but going beyond that would be difficult. In that case, the insurers might craft the endorsement to apply to a certain client only, instead of giving the law firm a blanket endorsement that would apply to every client of the firm.

Manuscript Endorsements—The Sky Is Indeed the Limit

Most of the optional endorsements discussed so far have been filed and approved by your states Department of Insurance. However, many states allow insurers to use "manuscript endorsements" to craft insurance policy language to meet the unique needs of individual law firms.

If your state allows insurers to use manuscript endorsements, then you can negotiate the exact language of each word of the endorsement with your insurer. As the endorsement name implies, the endorsement language is specifically written for you in a manner that is acceptable to both your law firm and your insurer.

95

These endorsements typically contain similar language as other optional endorsements, deleting entire sections of the policy and replacing them with language acceptable to both parties. If the change to the coverage policy form that your firm requests is covered under an already existing optional endorsement that has been approved by your states Department of Insurance, then your insurer will use that language. However, if the change to the coverage is out of the ordinary, then a "manuscript" endorsement is the way to go. Manuscript endorsements are not commonly used.

In addition, multiple authorizing persons working for an insurer usually needs to approve them, including underwriters and claims personnel. As such, it may take some time to negotiate a "manuscript" endorsement with an insurer.

Therefore, it is certainly your best bet to begin your reviewing your insurance policies about 90 days prior to your renewal to build in enough time to negotiate the coverage that you need.

The Truth—Size Matters

Your success in negotiating the exact coverage that you need is often dictated by the size of your law firm. Insurers are more willing to consider changes to their standard policy form language if a law firm is considered large enough.

Because optional endorsements are out of the normal workflow, some insurers will deny a request to add an optional endorsement because they simply don't want to take the time to do it given the premium that the carrier will earn. However, don't let this tendency dissuade you from asking for what you want.

The market for LPL insurance is usually very competitive. It is your firm's financial health and reputation that is on the line. A good LPL insurance policy should not be viewed as "good enough." It is worth your time to read the policy, ask for what you want, and realize the coverage that you need.

An expert LPL insurance broker is your advocate in this process and can greatly aid you in this process. So be as detailed as possible to allow the expert LPL insurance broker help craft coverage enhancements that you need and want as ultimately, it is your firm's responsibility to make sure that you have great coverage in place.

PEOPLE
just like
YOU

your best friends

T here's a lot of money involved in buying insurance overall and you want to make sure it works for you. Don't trust the financial protection of your firm to an insurance broker who is not a specialist in the problems you face every day.

Huge Industry

I nsurance is a huge industry. There's insurance for everything. Anything you can have, do, own, or manage—there's insurance for it and no one insurance broker can specialize in all of it. In fact, a professional independent insurance broker can only specialize in a few niches and really understand them.

Insurance is a very technical business. Policies, coverage, endorsements, exclusions—it has a language all its own. And the insurance needs of each industry are highly specific. Just because someone specializes in insuring homes or autos or huge manufacturing concerns, doesn't mean they know anything about the special needs of lawyers. And just because your wife's cousin sells insurance, doesn't mean he or she is the guy or gal with whom you want to trust the financial health of your practice!

Let's look at a few other things that you are NOT looking for:

♦ An insurance broker who tries to sell you their services on meaningless platitudes like "quality" or "excellence." Those are just buzzwords that mean very little.

♦ An insurance broker who tries to sell you on their services because they've "been around since 1974" or some such nonsense. Yes, you want a professional that has thoroughly studied the business, but what do you care what they were doing in 1974? Believe me, insurance back then wasn't anything like it is today.

♦ An insurance broker who doesn't know lawyers and law firms. We've said it before and I'll say it again: You wouldn't want a skin doctor to perform surgery on your heart, would you? we didn't think so. So don't trust your financial well-being to just any insurance broker!

Over the long haul, you'll be in a much better position when your insurance broker is not only a legal practice insurance specialist, but also is intimately familiar with all of the ups and downs and ins and outs of being a business owner on a day-to-day basis. We speak the same language!

The Fringe Benefits

Not only are we are legal-profession insurance specialists, not only are we fellow business owners, but there's more. We have a personal passion for business and business growth. We are national speakers on marketing—marketing that works for any kind of business, which means it can work for *your* practice. We possess a wealth of knowledge in this particular area. Not saying this to brag, but what should be of interest to you is that you can

Chapter 10

MIKE CARROLL & RJON ROBINS HELP ME SLEEP LIKE A BABY, AT NIGHT!

get more value from a fellow business owner who has studied marketing and knows how to help you grow your business.

Because we have a passion for marketing and growing a business, we're happy to be able to freely share the knowledge we have. Whatever the need—from tax information, to employer handbooks, to employment agreements, to how to joint venture with others in your community—we can help in all of these areas and more. We make any and all of these resources available to all our clients.

Lead by Example

Additionally, we lead by example. The strategies that we share are strategies we use myself in our own business. We have legal firms from all over who continually express their sincere appreciation for the ideas we've given them in the past. This is particularly true for those who are poised and ready to take their practice up to the next level.

We don't think in terms of nine to five—no more than you do as a lawyer. Our phones are answered by a live person 24/7. We think in terms of how a good lawyer works and operates. Claims don't happen within regular business hours and we're available to our clients whenever.

Some Final Words

There you have it. We're sorry that we've had to take you on a journey through the unthinkable and the unimaginable and bring things to your attention you may never have before considered, things you don't really want to think about. But they're real, they're out there and we want to see you get to the place where you never have to worry about, or be concerned about such matters. That confidence will free you up to do what you do best—operate your practice and make it a rip-roaring success.

Thank you for investing your time to learn more about how a legal insurance specialist works, and how it can benefit you in your business. We know your time is valuable, so we trust this was a helpful experience that will change forever how you look at possible practice disasters and catastrophes.

If you have questions, want further information, or want help in growing your business, please contact:

RJon Robins: rjon@howtomanageasmalllawfirm.com
Michael Carroll: michael@insuringlawyer.com

About the Authors

In 2016 How To MANAGE a Small Law Firm, the national outside managing partner services company that RJon Robins founded, was named by Inc. Magazine, for the second year in a row, as one of the 5,000 fastest growing privately held companies in the Country. Fastest in the category of helping solo and small law firm owners kick-butt and build better law firms (affording them more financial resources and freedom of time to help more clients and have a better life).

But. . .in 2008 RJon Robins lost pretty much everything. Which is pretty ironic because for 8 years previous, he'd made quite a great name for himself as one of the most trusted resources in the Country. Thousands of lawyers turned to him for help whenever they needed clarity about how to grow and manage their solo and small law firms. RJon first achieved notoriety after struggling with his own solo law firm which he (rather naively) went into it *without a written business plan*, without a written marketing plan, without written processes or procedures, without job descriptions for staff (who ate him out of house & home), and no financial controls to see what was happening before it was too late.

The notoriety didn't come from the failure of RJon's law firm serving his financial, personal and/or professional hopes, dreams or aspirations. That alone would have hardly distinguished him from about half a million other struggling

solo lawyers from all walks of life, who tilt at windmills all day long (without anyone to be managing partner), in every area of practice, all around the Country.

What brought the notoriety was a stroke of luck. RJon was in the right place at the right time and happened to say just the right thing, to just the right person; leading to RJon learning how to turn his struggling law firm around. On the strength of that, he was recruited by The Florida Bar's legendary J.R. Phelps of the world-famous Law Office Management Assistance Service (LOMAS). RJon invested the next four years of his career learning from the best (and from some of the worst) about what it takes to start, grow, save, salvage, and run a perfectly good law firm into the ground. He also learned quite a bit about how to do things the right way and used these skills, experiences, and profound insights to help thousands of lawyers build better law firms and lives. He helped some of them start and build highly-successful law firms that run like real businesses and helped others save, salvage and avert total disaster when the long term effects of running their law firm like a noble hobby finally hit home with a big, loud "splotch". As the only lawyer in the history of The Florida Bar to serve as a full time Small Law Practice Management Advisor, RJon spent the years between 1999-2001 working with what The Florida Bar estimates was more than 9,000 solo and small law firm owners.

Nowadays when he's not conducting CLE workshops around the Country on behalf of some of the biggest names in the legal industry (LexisNexis, Microsoft, Law Pay, Ruby Receptionists and dozens and dozens and dozens of bar associations, but who's counting), RJon is attending to his duties as CEO of the leading provider of outside managing partner, outside COO, and outside CFO services exclusively for solo and small law firms nationwide. . .or he's out practicing what he preaches about letting your business give you a life instead of the other way around.

Oh yeah, and RJon is a Member of The Florida Bar, where he's still authorized to appear before the Southern District Federal Court, as well as a member of The Association of Certified Fraud Examiners. RJon earned an interdisciplinary degree from The American University in Washington, DC (Communications, Law, Economics & Government), he graduated from Nova Southeastern College of Law and he doesn't eat ice cream every day but when he does, he prefers butter pecan.

Michael Carroll was born in Bangor, Maine. His family moved to Toledo, Ohio, when he was a small child and there he still resides with his bride of over 28 years, Cheryl (Sisinyak) Carroll, and four children, Catie, Patrick, Keandre, and Joey.

Mike has spent the last thirty years helping to protect Lawyers and Law Firms. He is considered a specialist in his field of insurance and one can quickly sense his passion for the service he provides and the message he has to share with Lawyers and Law Firms all around the country.

In September, 2016, and for the sixteenth consecutive year, the Carroll Insurance Group LLC and its subsidiary, Insuring Lawyer, was selected as a *Best Practices Agency*. This insurance company qualified for this status by ranking among the top performers in the annual Best Practices Study conducted by the Independent Insurance Agents & Brokers of America (IIABA) and Reagan Consulting. They were placed in the Best Practices Top 200 out of 37,500 independent agencies nationally. This is the equivalent to being in the top-five football program, year in and year out or like being a perennial Super Bowl contender.

Insuring Lawyer has offices in Maumee, Ohio, which is a suburb of Toledo, and in Phoenix, Arizona. Mike travels all over the country—he loves to travel—to meet many of his favorite people—lawyers just like you!

BRUCE HIGDON began his cartooning career at age 14, when he sold his first editorial cartoon to the local newspaper, and continued during his years at Middle Tennessee State University and as a Second Lieutenant in the United States Army. Upon retirement from the Army, Higdon continued his funny business as a writer for the Pentagon Speaker's Bureau, comedy monologue writer, and cartoonist and caricature artist for a variety of newspapers and magazines in the U.S., Germany and Canada. He also worked for CBS television as a courtroom artist. Today, he lives in his native Murfreesboro, Tennessee, from where he continues to draw his cartoons and caricatures for his Canadian and U.S. clients in his home studio. Four times during the year, he heads out to various locales, including combat areas, for the USO, to entertain our military. Higdon is a long-time member of the National Cartoonists Society, The Reserve Officers Association, and the Military Officers Association of America.

His website is www.punderstatements.com